NOTE TO READERS

HOW to be tHe BEST @everything

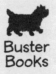

Buster
Books

First published in Great Britain in 2004 by Buster Books,
an imprint of Michael O'Mara Books Limited
9 Lion Yard
Tremadoc Road
London SW4 7NQ

A CIP catalogue record for this book is available from the
British Library.

ISBN 1-904613-89-6

10 9 8 7 6 5 4 3 2 1

www.mombooks.com/busterbooks

Printed and bound by Bookmarque Ltd, UK

Written by Dominique Enright
Illustrated by Niki Catlow
Edited by Samantha Barnes
Designed by Buster Books

Grateful thanks to Ellen Bailey; Claire Buchan; Jamie Buchan;
Toby Buchan; Agnieszka Chojnowska; David Bann; Ray King; Dr
John L. Breen of the School of Oriental and African Studies,
University of London; and to the press offices of the London
embassies of Greece, Sweden, and the Russian Federation.

CONTENTS

HOW TO DO AN OLLIE

This technique is the basis for most other skateboarding tricks. It allows a skater to jump over an obstacle, or on to a step or low wall, while the whole time the board appears to stick to the skater's feet.

① As you skate, place your back foot on the tail of the board, and your front foot halfway between the nose and the tail.

② Lower your centre of gravity by crouching in readiness to jump. Push down on the tail of the board with your back foot.

③ Now straighten your legs, effectively jumping into the air. The downward force on the tail will make the board come up with your front foot.

④ As the board rises slide your front foot to the nose. Then, with that foot, push down on the nose.

⑤ Lift your other foot to allow the tail to rise as the downward force is applied to the nose.

⑥ The board will now be level as you reach the peak of the jump. Then gravity takes hold and you and the board come down. As you descend, bend your legs again so as to take up the impact of landing.

9

HOW TO FLY A HELICOPTER

A helicopter can move up and down, forwards and backwards, and sideways. It can also rotate 360 degrees, stop in mid-air and hover... and while hovering it can spin round. As a helicopter pilot you must be at your most alert to be able to operate and control the movement of the craft.

① In one hand you have the collective pitch stick. This adjusts the main rotors so that the chopper can go up and down. It also controls the engine speed.

② In the other hand you have the cyclic pitch. This control makes the main rotor tilt so that it can pull the helicopter backwards, forwards or sideways.

③ Your feet rest on pedals that control the tail rotor, which allows the helicopter to turn to face any direction.

To perfect your flight and avoid embarrassing wild spins, dips this way and that and jerky rises and drops in the air, you have to make sure that your hands and feet work together to make the helicopter do what you want it to do.

HOW TO INSULT SOMEONE AND GET AWAY WITH IT

With this list of posh put-downs you'll never be short of something to say to unsuspecting friends and family, and you'll never get into trouble. Even your teacher will be flabbergasted.

asinine (ass-in-ine) very stupid: 'That was an asinine thing to do.'

blatherskite (blather-skite) a person who talks a load of nonsense: 'What a blatherskite you are!'

cacophony (ka-koff-funny) unpleasantly loud noise: 'What a cacophony my sister is making with her singing!'

discombobulate (dis-kom-bob-u-late) confuse: 'He was totally discombobulated by what I said.'

lollapalooza (lolla-palooza) a particularly attractive or impressive thing or person: 'He's no lollapalooza in his school uniform.'

noisome (noy-some) stinking, extremely unpleasant: 'My brother's bedroom is very noisome.'

tawdry (tordry) something flashy but of rubbish quality: 'Auntie, what fabulously tawdry jewellery you are wearing!'

technophobe (tekno-fobe) someone who dislikes or fears new technology: 'My dad can't even answer his mobile phone. He's a real technophobe.'

temerity (tim-erity) extreme boldness and cheek: 'What temerity to insult people like this!'

HOW TO SURVIVE IN SPACE

If you're very rich you could go to space for a holiday. The second way to get to space is to become an astronaut, and an astronaut must be the best at everything.

You have to wear a spacesuit while travelling on the space shuttle, but on the space station you can wear ordinary clothing. You'll spend time on board the space station growing plants, making crystals and performing experiments in near-zero gravity.

You will need to exercise frequently to reduce the loss of bone and muscle mass caused by weightlessness. Gym equipment is provided. During your free time, you can send e-mails home, play cards with fellow astronauts and admire the view of earth.

You will eat in the galley. The food is in containers attached to a tray which is in turn attached either to you or to a wall (otherwise your meal floats off). The meals themselves are not made up of tablets, though – you get proper appetizing food just like at home.

You will sleep in bunk-style sleeping quarters or, if there's not much room, in sleeping bags. These of course have to be attached to a wall or they will float about and you'll wake up in another part of the station.

As there's no washing machine aboard, you will need to take with you a great deal of clothing. Dirty clothes are sealed in plastic bags, in much the same way as all the rubbish is.

The toilet is fairly similar to those on earth. A steady flow of air moves through the unit when it is in use, carrying wastes to a special container or into plastic bags. The plastic bags are then sealed. (Some of the waste might be returned to earth for laboratory analysis.)

To wash, you will have a freshwater hose to shower you and a vacuum hose to suck up all the water. In other words you use vacuum cleaners on yourself! You can't have a bath as the water will float about. This is very dangerous as it might short-circuit electrical equipment.

As for brushing your teeth – that can be a challenge, too. You have to make sure the toothpaste is well down on the bristles and you have to stop the water from running away.

You may have to perform spacewalks to complete your mission. This will involve getting into a spacesuit, which has been made to withstand flying debris and to protect astronauts from dramatic temperature changes (from -85 °C in the shade to over 120 °C in the hot sunlight). It has a pressurized atmosphere, a source of oxygen and a means of removing carbon dioxide, a temperature regulator, some protection against radiation, and the means to communicate at all times with ground control or the space station. After going through depressurization procedures in the airlock, you'll step out. You are either attached by an air hose to the space station or you have a gas-propelled chair or unit that you can control so that you can go where you want rather than in space's random directions.

HOW TO LOSE YOUR HEAD

You will need a chair and table to sit at, with your homework set out on the table. You must be wearing a large shirt with buttons down the front and a collar.

(1) Sit down and unbutton your shirt. Pulling it up, rebutton the top three buttons behind your neck, with your head poking forward. Make sure that your shirt is firmly tucked into your trousers at the back. Shape the collar of your shirt into a neck-shaped circle.

(2) Still sitting on your chair, tuck your head under the table. With your free hand make sure that the front of your shirt collar is at least level with the tabletop, preferably above it. Make sure, too, that the collar is still in a roughly neck-shaped circle.

(3) Now put your elbows up onto the edge of the table. Pick up your pen in one hand, look busy and wait for people to come in and see how your homework has made you lose your head!

Think of other times when you can make a headless appearance. It can be very amusing at mealtimes, or at a friend's party!

HOW TO MAKE A MAGIC CIRCLE

The magic circle, or Möbius strip, named after a German mathematician, is a loop with only one surface and one edge. Impossible? Well, here is how you make one:

① Cut a strip of paper (try to keep the width even so that you have a long, thin rectangle). To make sure you tape the loop the right way, write A on the top right-hand corner, B on the top left, C on the bottom right, and D on the bottom left.

② Hold the two ends in your hands, give the strip a half-twist and tape together the ends, A to D, B to C. Now you have your loop.

③ Now take a pen and, starting at any point, draw a line along the centre of the strip, continuing all the way until you reach your starting point. You have drawn a line on both sides of the loop – but without lifting your pen or crossing any edge. The paper has only one side!

④ Now take a highlighter and colour the edge of the strip. You'll find that both edges are coloured. There is only one edge!

⑤ Now, with scissors, cut the Möbius strip along the central line that you drew earlier. It does not, as you'd expect, fall apart into two separate loops – instead you now have a single, larger one-sided loop!

⑥ Draw a central line around the resulting loop and cut along it – can you predict what will happen?

HOW TO FIGHT OFF A CROCODILE

Crocodiles are efficient killing machines. They might seem slow, *but* they can move very quickly in the water and leap out very suddenly and at great speed.

① If you're standing near a lake and a crocodile springs from the water towards you – run. And keep running for at least 15m (50ft). If you cannot run, try to get up on to the creature's back and stand on its neck to stop it from opening its jaws – crocodiles have weak jaw-opening muscles and you can hold their jaws shut without too much difficulty. On the other hand, their jaw-closing muscles are incredibly powerful and it is almost impossible to prise them open.

② Alternatively, you're in the water and a crocodile unexpectedly surfaces. You cannot outswim it, *but* if you can grab its jaws before it opens them, you have a chance of keeping its jaws shut (this assumes there's no part of you between them). Yell for help.

③ If the crocodile has clamped its jaws on one of your limbs, try to reach for a stick or anything else to use as a weapon and hit its sensitive nose repeatedly and poke it in the eyes. (A man actually managed to make a crocodile let go of his arms by biting its nose as hard as he could.) It might just back off, but they are quick, and you'll have to keep fighting until you're safe. Carry on yelling.

④ As a last resort, play dead. Crocodiles shake their prey to drown it but will stop when they think it's dead, and wedge the body in their pantry to have for dinner. Make your escape when it moves off.

HOW TO BE A VIP

If you are very important, you must know very important people. So impress your friends. When you're out with them, greet any stranger you pass by in the street who looks as though he or she might have some kind of status. Quite often the person will say 'Hello' back thinking that you're the child of someone they know. 'Who's that?' your friends will ask. 'Oh, that's Lady So-and-so, an old friend of ours,' or 'That's Sir Henry. He owes me a favour – that's why he pretended not to see me. I'm going to have to call him,' or 'That was DJ Dingbat. He's always asking me what CDs to buy.' And so on. Don't overdo it – your friends will catch on. But get it right and they'll be full of respect.

HOW TO SWIM FREESTYLE

So you want to ditch the doggy paddle? The fastest and most impressive-looking swimming stroke is the freestyle (also called the front crawl).

Body and head: Your body should be straight and streamlined, with no arms and legs sticking out, and your hips in line with your shoulders. It helps to keep your face in the water, looking down at the bottom of the pool. Only move your head when you need to take a breath. As you swim try to keep all of your body close to the surface of the water.

Legs: Use these to keep you up and maintain your balance as well as to propel you along. Try to make long, fast kicks, ensuring that the whole length of each leg is moving up and down. Bend your knees slightly and splash only a little with your feet. Try counting to six quickly and kicking your legs alternately in time with this.

It is important to keep your legs close together (but of course not so close that they move as one).

Arms: They are your main source of power. Stretch one arm in front of your head as far as you can, close to the surface of the water, letting your shoulders and hips follow. Then slice your hand down through the water, thumb first, splashing as little as possible. Keep your fingers together, forming a shallow scoop to help push through the water. As you bring your arm down, bend your elbow and push your hand towards your feet, your fingers following a path down the middle of your chest and stomach. When you bring the arm back up to repeat this stroke, try to lift your elbow out of the water first.

Keeping your hand near the water surface and close to your body, move it forward to the start position in front of your head.

The second arm should follow the first so that it is about to go down in front of you as the first is coming up. With some practise you'll slip into the rhythm of the alternating strokes, your hips and shoulders rolling slightly to the left or the right as you stretch each hand forward.

Breathing. Your face is in the water, so you must remember to turn your head when you want to take a breath. Turn it as smoothly as you can, leaving the side of your head resting in the water. An effective method is to turn your head to the left to breathe when your right arm is outstretched and to bring your head round to the right to breathe again as you stretch out your left arm.

You should now be able to kick, pull and breathe. Keep your legs kicking all of the time and your arms following each other. Get into the habit of breathing regularly, every two, three or four arm strokes. And try to avoid splashing too much – it's not professional.

HOW TO SPOOK YOUR FAMILY

Could your house be haunted? It could be if you have anything to do with it ...

Every morning, your family come downstairs to find that the table has been laid – and that one chair is pulled out, and there's tea in the cup at that place, as though someone had been sitting there and just got up from the table moments before ... But there's no one there.

Things move. However often your mother puts that vase of flowers on the mantelpiece, the next time she comes into the room, it is back on the table. And that's not the only thing that moves. Furniture, too, appears to have moved by itself during the night.

The dog whines and scrabbles at the never-used door to the cellar (or spare room, broom cupboard, etc.). Nobody knows why – except you – you know his favourite chew toy is hidden behind it.

Every night, when everybody is asleep, lights go on, found in the morning by whoever is first to get up. (Make sure no one hears you get up in the night.)

One particular door seems always to open by itself (the one to which you can attach a bit of thread without its being spotted).

Clothes that have been scattered about all appear neatly folded in a pile. But other clothes disappear from their drawers to reappear in someone else's.

Other things seem to have moved. The tins in the

cupboard are stacked, their labels swapped, and the eggs in the fridge are hard boiled. And the chocolate keeps disappearing!

Footsteps, music and talking are heard from another part of the house, but there's no one there. (Keep whatever machinery you use to record and play sounds well hidden.)

HOW TO MAKE A STINK

Other than the most obvious way, that is ...

Although you can buy traditional stink bombs you can make something that smells just as bad very cheaply and easily.

You will need: an egg, a drop of milk, half a teaspoon of sugar and a tin or plastic food container with a lid that can be shut tight. If plastic, it ought to be made of bendy rather than rigid plastic, which could crack with the pressure of the noxious gas.

(1) Break the egg into the container, add the milk and sugar and shut your container tight. Put it in a warm place, preferably outdoors – somewhere that gets a lot of sun. If it has to be indoors, hide it near a boiler or radiator. Leave it for about two weeks.

(2) After two weeks use a suitable instrument to make about 20 holes in the lid of the container.

(3) Now find a good place to hide your creation. Soon a delightful stink will be wafting out, and you can enjoy watching everyone wandering about sniffing and looking for the source of the revolting smell.

HOW TO GIVE MOUTH-TO-MOUTH RESUSCITATION

Mouth-to-mouth resuscitation could save a person's life. Many types of injury can cause someone to stop breathing, and if this happens, a person has little time before they suffer permanent brain damage or death. Don't practise on a person who is breathing – it can be dangerous, so use a doll.

1. Check to see if the casualty is breathing. If he's not, quickly check to see if there is any blockage in the air passages – including his tongue. Use your fingers to remove any obstruction you find. Call an ambulance.

2. Now check again as the removal of a blockage may have started him breathing again.

3. If not, put him on his back. Loosen his clothing.

4. Tilt his head well back by lifting his chin. Hold him firmly by the chin and by the top of the head. Make sure his airway (the passage in the throat) is clear.

5. Hold his head and pinch his nostrils shut between your finger and thumb.

6. Take a deep breath, and then seal your lips firmly round his mouth. Breathe out steadily into his mouth. His chest should rise (if it doesn't it means there's a blockage to be removed – quickly!). Remove your mouth, watch the chest fall, and then blow into his mouth again.

7. Check for breathing and check the pulse by placing your first two fingers on the underside of his wrist.

⑧ Continue the pattern of blowing into the casualty's mouth and watching his chest rise and fall for 12 breaths. Check again, and if he hasn't started breathing by himself continue until he does or until help arrives.

⑨ If he's started breathing place him in the recovery position. Place the arm closest to you straight out from the body. Lift and bend his far arm at the elbow, resting it against the near cheek. Grab and bend his far knee and then, protecting the head with one hand, gently roll the person towards you by pulling the far knee over and to the ground. Stay close until help arrives.

HOW TO PLAY THE TOILET ROLL

A kazoo is one of the world's simplest musical instruments. To make one you will need: a cardboard tube (from a roll of kitchen paper, clingfilm, foil or toilet roll), greaseproof paper, an elastic band, scissors, ruler, pencil, and coloured pens or paint to decorate.

① Start by decorating your tube (this is optional, but who wants to be seen playing the toilet roll?).

② That done, cut a square, 12x12cms (5x5ins), of greaseproof paper.

③ Place the greaseproof paper over one end of the tube and secure it with the elastic band.

④ Hum or sing into the open end. The greaseproof paper vibrates to give a buzzing sound that enhances the sound you make.

HOW TO SERVE LIKE A WIMBLEDON CHAMPION

You have complete control of the shot as it starts with you. Keep calm and take the time to get into position. At all times, remember: balance, timing and rhythm.

① Grip the racket, spreading your fingers around the handle without squeezing too hard. Keep your arm relaxed. Take the ball in the other hand.

② Facing the net, point your racket at where you want the ball to go and use your throwing hand (left for most) to support it lightly.

③ Raise your hands together just a short way, then bring them down together. As you do this start to turn your body so that you are sideways to the court. At the same time transfer your weight from your front foot to your back foot. Try to keep this sequence of movements smooth and co-ordinated.

④ Raise your throwing arm (left if you're playing right-handed) into an upright position to release the ball above your head. A good height to throw the ball is about 15cm (6ins) above your normal reach. Keep your arm straight to help throw the ball accurately and make sure you don't release the ball too soon – it will fly at an angle towards the net and force you to lean forward to hit it.

⑤ While the ball is in the air you need to bring the racket fluidly back and up and ready to hit the ball. This is probably the most difficult part of the action, because at the same time as co-ordinating your arms you also need to transfer your weight from your back foot on to your front.

⑥ As the ball gets to the top of the throw, direct the racket at the ball in a swift throwing action. Aim to hit the ball at full stretch, with your racket arm straight, at the highest point you can reach it. The higher you make contact the more power you can generate and the harder and faster the ball will go.

⑦ Follow through across your body, then look to recover quickly ready for your next shot.

HOW TO GET RID OF HICCUPS

Swallow a teaspoon of sugar,

or gulp down a glass of water,

or eat a piece of dry bread slowly,

or gargle water,

or drink water from the farthest side of the glass rim,

or hold your breath and count backwards,

or try all these at once – you'll probably feel so ill and confused that you'll forget about your hiccups.

HOW TO MUMMIFY AN ANCIENT EGYPTIAN

You are an ancient Egyptian, working as an embalmer. The family of a rich noblewoman who has recently died, come to you. They wish to preserve her body to make sure her soul has somewhere to reside during the afterlife.

① First, using special custom-made hooks and spoons, you draw out the brain through the nose. This is very tricky, as you have to be careful not to damage the face.

② You then take out the internal organs (the lungs, liver, stomach, intestines and so on), through a cut made in the left side of the tummy. The heart, however, you leave where it is.

③ Your helpers then wash the body in spiced palm wine.

④ When that's done, you cover the body, packing it inside as well as out (especially all round the heart), with natron, a mineral salt found in dried lake beds. You leave the natron there for 40 days to absorb all the moisture from the body. In the meantime you have been treating the removed organs in the same way. These used to be stored in special 'canopic' jars and buried alongside the mummy;

you, however, use the new practice of preserving them, wrapping them up and popping them back into the body.

⑤ After 40 days, the body should be completely dried out, and look shrivelled and wrinkled. You clean away the natron and rub oils into the skin to soften it. You pad out the body with strong-smelling herbs and spices, mud, sawdust, rags and other bits of linen to stop it from sinking in and losing its shape. That done, you pop out the eyes and replace them with false ones.

⑥ Wrapping-up time can take many days as there are 20 layers of linen strips – hundreds of metres – to wind round the body. As you wind the bandages round the mummy you slip in various charms, made of precious metals and precious stones, among the linen strips. On some of the bandages you write prayers and magic words. You use resin glue to keep the bandages in place.

⑦ As your current customer is from a noble family, you have been asked to place a gold-leaf-covered mask over the almost fully bandaged head. (You made sure that the mask-maker managed a reasonable likeness of the dead noblewoman before you bound up the head.) Now you notice with approval that he has made her eyes bigger and nose smaller than they were in life – she might as well be more beautiful in the afterlife than she was in the life she has just left.

⑧ Your job is done, and you hand the mummy over to the specialist craftsmen who have been working on her coffin and tomb.

HOW TO SURVIVE A VOLCANIC ERUPTION

First of all, know what you are up against. Deep down below the surface of the earth, a build-up of gases and the movement of the crustal plates increase pressure to a point where it can no longer be contained. The result is an explosion of boiling magma (molten rock) in the form of lava, flaming gases and red-hot fragments of rock and dust.

At any given time there are usually at least 12 volcanoes erupting somewhere in the world. If you find yourself living near one make sure you are prepared.

Stock up on provisions of bottled water, food, medical supplies, blankets, warm clothing and batteries in case power lines are cut. Collect water in your bath, sinks and containers as mains supplies may quickly become polluted.

In the event of an eruption, seek shelter at home and don't leave unless advised to by authorities. Keep listening to the radio or TV for news and advice.

If you go outside, wear a mask and goggles to keep volcanic ash out of your eyes and lungs. Keep gutters and roofs clear of settling ash, which could bring down the house upon you.

If possible, don't accidentally wander away from other people, and always remain on the trodden paths.

If you are caught outside during an eruption, be aware of the hazards that come with an eruption: the flying debris, hot gases, lava flows, explosions, mudslides, avalanches, boiling water sprays from geysers, and floods. If you are in an area that could experience a lava flow, be ready to outrun it and never try to cross it.

Look for hills and head towards them, they may afford you some protection from the destructive and devastating effects of the eruption.

HOW TO READ SOMEONE'S MIND

(1) Ask a friend to pick a number between 1 and 10.

(2) Ask them to multiply that number by 9.

(3) Ask them to add the digits of the number they get.

(4) Now ask them to subtract 5 from their answer.

(5) Tell your friend to think of the letter in the alphabet that corresponds to their number (1 is A, 2 is B, 3 is C and so on).

(6) Tell them to think of a country in Europe that starts with that letter.

(7) Now ask them to think of an animal that starts with the last letter of that country.

(8) And then a colour that starts with the last letter of their animal.

(9) Now tell them that you know what they are thinking, and that it is an orange kangaroo in Denmark.

Chances are that you're right!

HOW TO WIN COMPUTER GAMES

It is a good idea to read the instruction manual and/or play the tutorial and pay attention to everything that happens in it. It is there to help you.

In shooting games:

- Snipe for preference (i.e. shoot from long distances with accurate, powerful guns).
- Aim for head shots.
- Zigzag/ keep behind cover to avoid being sniped yourself.
- Remember to reload during quiet points, preferably behind cover.
- Use appropriate weapons – for instance, for assaults you need automatic firing and big clips.
- Be careful not to waste ammo – only use lots of bullets when you are surrounded by enemies.
- Circle strafe (sidestep round enemies while shooting to avoid their aim).

In driving games, brake as you go round corners, and learn to use the handbrake.

In any games, if you know you're making the correct and only possible move, but it is apparently getting you nowhere, do persevere. It might be part of the game's programming that you have to make a certain number of attempts before you succeed.

Be alert at all times as you move through your game – watch out for anything that might have moved or any object that you don't remember seeing last time you were in that location.

Collect anything that can be picked up – even the most unlikely items will probably come in useful.

If you're playing against one or more players in the same room, keep an eye on your opponent(s). Take your cue from what they are doing. And do not allow yourself to be distracted, either by external events, or by your opponents' comments.

Taunting your opponents often throws them completely off their game, giving you a chance to beat them: 'That tree/rock/hill looked really dangerous – lucky you got it in time!'; 'You have to expect corners'; 'Oh dear, dear. I didn't realize you were a beginner!' And so on.

Or 'advice' can put them off their game – 'Careful – look behind you!'; 'Ooh, I wouldn't do that, if I were you'; 'Look, you see that rock there?... Oh, too late! What bad luck!'

HOW TO SEE THROUGH YOUR HAND

(1) Take a cardboard tube (from a roll of kitchen paper, clingfilm, or toilet paper) and look through it with your right eye.

(2) Place the edge of your left hand against the tube with its palm facing you.

(3) With both eyes open, stare at the point where the tube and the edge of your hand meet and you'll see that you have a hole in your hand.

HOW TO WRITE A QUICK POEM

A homework topic that usually provokes groans starts with the words, 'Write a poem about...' If the topic is *boring* it's even harder to be creative, but here is a quick, unfailing way to impress your teachers and be the envy of friends.

① On line one, write the subject (say you've been told to write about a storm): 'Storm'.

② On line two, write down two descriptive words that spring to your mind when you think of storms: 'Dark, angry'.

③ On line three, write three verbs connected to a storm: 'Blows, howls, crashes'.

④ On line four, write a thought that comes to you: 'Will it never end'.

⑤ On line five, write another phrase to describe the subject (i.e. storm): 'Nature's rage'.

⑥ Storm.   OR: Me.
   Dark, angry,   Modest but wonderful,
   Blows, howls, crashes.   I can, I know and I do.
   Will it never end,   The best at everything,
   Nature's rage?   That's me!

You will soon do much better than this. And then, if you like, you can refine your new skill – make it rhyme or add more lines as you want. Soon your friends will be coming to you for help in writing messages in greetings cards!

HOW TO GET OUT OF QUICKSAND

Whatever you do, don't think of all those films in which a character is gradually sucked, struggling and screaming, into depths of quicksand, then vanishes from sight with a faint plop. Remind yourself instead that you can float on quicksand – it is in fact a lot easier to float on quicksand than in water.

(1) The worst thing to do is to thrash around and move your arms and legs through the mixture, you will only succeed in forcing yourself farther down into the quicksand.

(2) If you are heading to an area where you think there may be quicksand, including riverbanks, beaches and marshes, carry a stout stick. If you find yourself sinking in quicksand lay the stick down on the surface of the quicksand and gently slide onto it on your back. Your body weight will spread out across the stick and you will find it easier to float. If you don't have a stick, turn onto your back and slowly spread out your arms and legs to increase your surface area.

(3) Once afloat, move very slowly and carefully using your arms, and edge your way towards firm ground.

33

HOW TO MAKE A SIMPLE RAFT

You will need: 4 x straight wooden poles, about 182cm (6ft) long and 8–10cm (3–4ins) thick; 3 shorter wooden poles of the same thickness, but about 122cm (4ft) long; at least 61m (200ft) of 5-mm (³⁄₁₆-in) nylon cord; at least twelve strong 5-litre (1.1-gallon; 1.3 US gallons) empty rectangular plastic containers with screw tops, of the kind used for detergent; any planks or boards, at least 182cm (6ft) long, that you can find; nails, hammer, screwdriver, and scissors or a knife.

① Lay the end of one of the shorter poles over the end of a longer one and at right angles to it, and lash together. Lay the other end of the shorter pole over the end of a second longer one, and lash together; then lash the free ends of the two longer poles under each end of a second shorter one – creating a rectangular structure.

② Lash each end of the third shorter pole across and over the middle of the two longer ones; then lash the third and fourth long poles beneath the middle of the three shorter crossways poles – the distance between these two long poles should be just wider than the narrowest side of one of the empty containers. You should now have a rectangle consisting of four long poles crossed by three shorter ones laid on top of them.

③ Now lash three of the empty 5-litre containers at even intervals along the inside of one of the long poles, the top pointing towards the stern (rear) of the raft. Repeat along the inside of the other long side pole, and then again between the two centre long poles.

④ Launch the raft in shallow water and test its buoyancy – ideally, deck level should be about 15cm (6ins) above the surface of the water when a person is sitting on the raft. If necessary, lash more containers to the long poles (you can get six containers along each pole) until you achieve the right degree of buoyancy. But remember to allow for the fact that you will be adding more weight when you fix the decking, which will make the raft sit lower in the water.

⑤ Now fix your decking of boards or planks to the three shorter cross poles – you can lash them in place, or otherwise nail or screw them to the cross poles. There can be gaps between the deck planks – in fact, the lighter you build your raft, the better it will float and the easier it will be to get in and out of the water. The decking planks don't need to touch each other.

⑥ Relaunch the raft and climb aboard.

⑦ If the raft is floating well, you can add other structures – a guard-rail of poles lashed to uprights all the way round, for instance; a rudder (a paddle or short oar lashed to an upright at the stern in such a way that it can be moved from right to left works well); a mast (and pirate flag of skull-and-crossbones); even a small cabin if the raft is buoyant enough.

A useful knot for putting together a raft is the square lashing, which you could learn how to lash from any book of knots, or from articles on the Internet.

HOW TO TEACH A PARAKEET TO TALK

To ensure you have a bird with the ability to talk, and one that you can train, choose a young male Australian parakeet, or an English, Ringnecked, Alexandrine or Plumheaded parakeet.

Parakeets develop their communication skills by talking to each other, so if you can, keep two or three birds. If not, a useful trick is to put a mirror in your bird's cage. This will cheer him up and he will chat happily with his own reflection just as if it were another bird in the cage. Be sure to remove the mirror when you start teaching the parakeet to talk – or he may prefer to talk to himself!

To train your bird, first you must make friends with him – spend time with him, talk to him, keep his cage clean, give him plenty of clean water and make sure he is well fed. Train him to sit on your hand or finger.

To teach him to talk, speak clearly and slowly, repeating the word or phrase over and over. Parakeets tend to speed up words when they repeat them, so speak slowly and your parakeet will pronounce the word correctly.

Parakeets can recognize and pick up certain sounds better than others.

They are best with consonants such as d, k, t, p or b. A traditional phrase such as 'Hello, how are you?' isn't very good to start with, since it is hard for the bird to say.

It is important to speak to your parakeet regularly and to speak to him for more than a few minutes – if possible make your training session at least half an hour a day.

During lessons, cover the top and three sides of his cage with a towel or cloth, so that he is not distracted from you or your voice.

Don't move on to a second word or phrase until he can repeat the first one. Be patient; once he has learnt a few words, it will take much less time to learn more.

Once a parakeet learns to repeat words, you can teach him to recognize an object and say its name, like a book or pen. Simply hold the object up to the bird and repeat the word.

After a while you can train your bird to recognize you by your name (or whatever you choose to call yourself). 'Good morning, Boss!' your bird might greet you. But be careful not to refer to any of your family members by nicknames you would prefer to keep secret in front of your new talkative pet!

HOW TO HOOT WITH YOUR HANDS

(1) Imagine a cave with only one small entrance – that cave is formed from your clasped hands, while the entrance is the slit between your thumbs. There are two ways for you to make this cave:

a) Clasp your hands together, with the fingers of one hand (hand A) folded over the other (hand B) between the thumb and first finger, and the fingers of hand B folded over the outside of hand A. Hand A's thumb rests lightly on hand B's. Now adjust your hands to form a little cave between them, with the two outer edges of your hands right against each other. Apart from the entrance to the cave make sure there are no gaps between the edges of your hands or any of your fingers, and make sure that the wrist edges of your hands are pressed together.

b) Instead of clasping your hands together, lace your fingers tightly together so there are no gaps for air to get through. Make sure the wrist edges of your hands are pressed tightly and then pull your palms away from each other, so as to form your cave.

(2) For either kind of cave, relax your thumbs so that they are lightly bent, with parts of the nails touching. Line up the upper part of your thumbs with the underside of your first finger. You will now have a slit – wider in the middle than the top or bottom – between your thumbs.

(3) Place your lips on your thumb knuckles, the upper lip brushing the bases of your thumbnails. Be very careful not to close the air hole with your lower lip – the air that

you are about to blow into your cave needs to come out.

④ Blow steadily – and not too hard – through your knuckles. If you're lucky you'll hear a raspy almost-hoot (if you're very lucky you might hear a kind of whistly hoot); if you're not so lucky you'll just hear a puffing sound. Adjust your fingers and thumbs carefully, make sure your cave is still sealed tight, and that the air that you are blowing through the top of the air hole is coming out through the bottom (you can probably feel it coming out). It can help to have damp, even wet, hands.

⑤ Keep trying. Sooner or later you will get a good hoot and, as you practise, it will become easier and the sound will become clearer. Then you can start experimenting with blowing harder or softer, bending and flexing your fingers and thumbs, squeezing your hands together, etc., to change the note.

HOW TO SPEAK IN CODE

EGGY-PEGGY: Add 'egg' before each vowel.
Example: 'Eggi eggam thegge beggest.' ('I am the best.')

GREE: Add 'gree' to the end of every word.
Example: 'Igree amgree thegree bestgree.'

NA: Add 'na' to the end of every word.
Example: 'Ina amna thena bestna.'

PIG LATIN: Move the first letter to the end of the word and add 'ay' to it.
Example: 'Iay maay hetay estbay.'

HOW TO KEEP PEOPLE IN SUSPENSE

A 'cliffhanger' is anything in a story, article, radio or TV programme, or film that leaves a listener, reader or viewer in suspense – the hero is left hanging from a cliff, in deadly danger of his life. It is a trick used to keep people's attention – by being kept in suspense, they want to know more, and so will read on, or keep listening or watching. ('Cliffhanger endings' are often used to make people buy the next edition of a magazine, or watch the next programme in a serial.) You can use similar tricks to become the best teller (or writer) of jokes, stories, and even speeches, and hold your audience in suspense:

① Don't give too much away too early. Quickly ending an account with something like 'Suddenly a lot of shots rang out and they all fell dead. The End' leaves readers or listeners disappointed and frustrated.

② Never rush. Spin the tale out (but don't go so slowly that it becomes boring). Pause occasionally – this often makes people say 'Go on!' or 'What happened next?'

③ Change direction. Just as you get to a good bit, say something like, 'Meanwhile, as the phantom bus bore down on us, Gran was making Eccles cakes at home . . .'

④ Break off your story occasionally. Then suddenly a

huge black shape appeared in front of him and he – oh, there goes the bell. Tell you later!'

⑤ Leave the best part to the end, but build the drama up bit by bit.

If you practise this technique, you will soon gain a reputation as a brilliant storyteller.

HOW TO MAKE A BALLOON DOG

① Blow up a long, skinny balloon, leaving about 3cm (1¼ins) of unblown balloon at the end.

② Tie a knot at the end of the balloon.

③ Make a twist in the balloon about 5cm (2ins) from the knotted end.

④ Make two more twists about 2½cm (1in) apart from each other, after the first twist. Make sure not to let go of the balloon.

⑤ Twist the two smaller bubbles together. These will become the ears. You will see that you have already made the dog's head.

⑥ Make three more twists about 5cm (2ins) apart and twist these sections together. These will be the neck and the two front legs.

⑦ Now, make three more twists, one for the dog's body, and two more about 5cm (2ins) apart for its back legs.

⑧ Fold and twist the two smaller sections together and twist the legs down.

HOW TO BUILD A CAMPFIRE

(1) Make sure you have the permission of the person who owns the land. Choose a suitable spot – away from anything that might catch fire, especially trees, bushes and buildings. Make sure that your belongings are out of the way and remove stones from the area, as these can get very hot and shatter explosively. It is a good idea to have a bucket of water or sand (or soil) close by in case your fire gets too enthusiastic.

(2) If the site for the fire is grassy, cut around and under a 1m (3¼ ft) square of turf. Lift it out, lay it right side up and sprinkle it with water. The grass should stay fresh until you replace it after you have broken camp. Make your fire in the space from which you lifted the turf.

(3) You will need three kinds of burnable material: tinder, kindling and fuel. Tinder is light stuff that catches fire easily – like shredded bark, dry grass or dry pine needles. Gather enough to half-fill a standard-size bucket.

(3) Kindling is slim, dry dead twigs – no thicker than a pencil. Collect at least enough to fill the same bucket.

(4) For fuel you will need firewood – dead, dry sticks thicker than kindling. Start by filling your bucket – you can collect more fuel as and when necessary. Make sure your fuel is neither green nor wet, as this will make the fire smoke.

(5) Make a heap of the tinder, then lean the kindling over it to build a triangular structure like a tepee; over this

place some of the firewood, also standing and leaning in. Too much fuel will stifle your fire – there should be plenty of air space beneath the kindling and fuel.

⑥ Light the tinder. If it takes, the kindling will catch fire too and as it burns more strongly the firewood should take.

⑦ You will soon have a merry little fire. But keep an eye on it – fire is sneaky. And when you have finished, make sure you put the fire out completely – not a single glowing ember should be left – spread the ashes out, and pour on some water to be on the safe side.

HOW TO TIE A TIE

① Lift up your shirt collar and put the tie round your neck so that both ends hang down at the front. The wide end should hang about 30cms (1ft) lower than the thin end; it can hang on the right or left, whichever you prefer.

② Cross the wide end over the thin end near the collar, then take it round underneath the thin end.

③ Bring the wide end over the thin end again and back underneath; then push it up through the back of the V-shape made by the partially formed knot.

④ Bring the wide end forward (i.e. away from you) through the V and down through the front loop of the knot.

⑤ Hold the knot with one hand and with the other gently pull on each end of the tie until the knot is tight.

⑥ Hold the thin end and slide the knot up to your neck, then fold your collar down.

HOW TO ANNOY YOUR BROTHERS AND SISTERS

With these tricks, your brothers and sisters will be so annoyed they'll be irritated just having you in the room! But beware of the consequences — don't do any of these things unless you're prepared for war!

Hang around when your brother or sister is lounging in front of the telly and, when you hear your parents approaching, quickly busy yourself tidying the room — you'll get endless praise from your parents, whilst your sibling will be frowned upon for his or her laziness. To keep yourself amused while you wait for your parents to see you working so hard, find as many excuses as possible for walking slowly past the TV screen and blocking your brother's or sister's view.

Tie a knot in one of your brother's pyjama legs. Do it on random nights so he never expects it, and always falls over with a thud.

If your brother or sister has the traditional two sheets and a bedspread or blanket on their bed, make an apple-pie bed (make sure you are around to see them get into bed). To do this, pull off the bedspread/blanket and tuck in the head end of the top sheet at the head of the bed, and cover it with the pillow. Then untuck the bottom end of the top sheet and fold it upwards so that it goes up to, and preferably slightly over, the pillows. Tidy all the folds and cover it with the bedspread so that it looks exactly as it always does.

If your brother or sister has a girlfriend or boyfriend, it's just too good an opportunity to miss; leave humiliating photos of them lying around throughout the house; bring up the subject of your many farting competitions over dinner; if there's an extension phone make burping sounds down the line when they talk to each other.

When your brother or sister is about to go out, make sure that whatever is most vital to him or her is missing. After ten minutes of furious searching, you will 'find' it; the first time you might be met with thanks, but your brother or sister will soon catch on and get very annoyed.

Get a TV guide and look up what is on at the same time as the soaps your sister watches every night, then tell your parents that you need to watch something on the other channel for school. Act totally bored by the programme whenever your parents are out of sight.

When you have to do homework together claim to need everything that they are using, the calculator, the ruler etc. Whilst you wait to 'use' these items, drum on the table, or hum to yourself. When they finally give up the item find something pointless to do with it – use the calculator to write the word 'shell' upside down (77345), and the ruler to underline your name on your notebook.

HOW TO GAG A KNOW-IT-ALL

'Did you know that your brain's 80 per cent water?'

(This is fact, not an insult.)

HOW TO TAKE A PENALTY KICK

You have three things to consider: the goalkeeper, how you kick the ball, and where you send the ball.

① **Goalkeeper**. The goalie's aim is first of all to distract you and put you off your kick. Check the goalie's position but don't pay him any other attention. If you look at the goalie, he's gained an advantage.

The goalie's second aim is to save the penalty, either by predicting which way you'll kick the ball or by waiting, following and stopping the ball.

② **Ball**. There are two favoured techniques for kicking the ball. One is to kick the ball hard with the laces of your boot – the advantage is that it's a powerful shot; the disadvantage is that there is more risk of the ball going wide or straight over the crossbar. The second technique is to kick the ball with the side of the foot, with less power but more accuracy.

③ **Aim**. Before kicking, select the spot where you wish to direct the ball, but do not look at this position and risk giving it away to the goalie. You might want to try tricking the goalie by approaching the ball as if you're going to kick it in one direction, but then kick it the other way, or by running up to the ball as though you are about to hit it hard with the laces of your boot, but instead use the side of your foot to place the ball to the right or the left.

The best odds are to aim high and preferably to the left or right, as a low centre shot stands less chance of getting past the goalie.

HOW TO HYPNOTIZE A CHICKEN

Rest assured that no chicken is hurt during this, not even its dignity is shaken (unless you can ask it to run around like a human when it is in the trance). This is one of several ways to lull a chicken into a stupor – just make sure you are gentle and quiet.

① Place the chicken on a table, laying it on its side with one wing under its body. Hold it down gently with its head flat on the surface.

② With one finger from your free hand repeatedly trace a straight line, about 30cm (1ft) long, in front of the bird's eyes – outwards from its beak-tip and along the table. Alternatively, take a piece of chalk (a colour that contrasts with the surface) and draw a 30-cm (1-ft) line from the beak-tip out in front of the bird. Hold the chicken still for a bit as it stares ahead along the line.

Soon it will be in a hypnotic trance. How long it remains in that trance varies from seconds to hours. But any sudden movement or noise will bring the bird to and with a squawk of surprise it'll be up and off and on its way.

47

HOW TO TREAT STINGS

You can recognize if a person is allergic to a sting if they have difficulty breathing, their pulse speeds up, they collapse or areas away from the sting swell up. In this case be sure immediately to call an ambulance, but also ask the person if they've got treatment with them (some carry adrenalin ready to be injected). Likewise if they've been very badly stung or have been stung in the mouth or eyes, call an ambulance at once.

Otherwise, when a person is stung, they will suffer only short-lived pain and some discomfort that can be soothed by pressing something cool on to the affected area or rubbing it with an ice cube.

For bee stings, first you must carefully pull out the sting with a pair of tweezers, gripping the sting where it's closest to the skin. Then, to soothe the pain, bathe the sore patch with a solution of bicarbonate of soda. Fresh wee also soothes, but your patient might object!

Wasps do not leave their sting behind. If you dab vinegar on the stung area, it will reduce the pain.

Jellyfish stings are painful but usually harmless (the dangerous one is the Portuguese Man-of-War, which you can recognize by its size and blue-mauve bladder that floats on the surface). Don't rub the stung area, but rinse it thoroughly. Calamine lotion will soothe it.

For nettle stings, rubbing with dock leaves provides the best relief, but although dock is common and often grows near nettles, you might not be able to find or identify it (a green-leaved weed with clusters of small greenish or reddish petal-less flowers), in which case you could try mint (recognizable by its scent).

HOW TO CLIMB A PALM TREE

You need to be barefoot to get a grip on the tree, but wear a long-sleeved shirt and trousers to protect yourself from a bad scraping.

Climb like a frog: flex your legs on each side of the tree with the soles of your feet firmly against the sides of the trunk. Your legs should look like those of a frog, bent knees sticking out either side of you. Move one hand up, against the other side of the trunk and place the other hand at chest level on your side of the tree. Move yourself up by straightening your legs, shifting your weight to your hands and, with a jump-like motion, bringing up both of your feet at the same time to return to the frog position, progressing up the tree as you do so. Rest after each few 'jumps'. When you can reach the palm leaves, grab hold and make your way up to the coconuts.

Going down: either return to the frog-like position, feet first, and jump down step-by-step, or lower your hands one by one behind the trunk while allowing the soles of your feet to slide down against the trunk.

HOW TO BE FIRST OFF THE STARTING BLOCK

(1) As you wait for the starter's commands, breathe gently and try to relax – to help your body run efficiently and quickly.

(2) **'On your marks.'** Crouch on one knee and place your hands just behind the starting line, forming a high bridge between your fingers and thumbs. Your hands should be placed slightly further apart than your shoulders. Keep your eyes fixed on the ground ahead of you to help your balance, focus and relaxation. Try not to allow anything to distract you.

(3) **'Set.'** Raise your hips so they're just higher than your shoulders. Keep your head at a comfortable angle – don't try to look up at the track but don't look right down either. Lean your body as far forward as you can and aim to begin running without stumbling. Breathe in. Be ready for the starting signal.

(4) **'Go!'** Breathe out hard and pump your arms and legs. To start with try not to take too big strides, wait until you're balanced and are running rhythmically. Thrust your elbows as high as possible with each backward swing and drive your legs with a high knee action.

(5) Keep going, and leave everyone else behind!

HOW TO PLAY A TRICK ON THE WHOLE CLASS

Before you play your trick, enlist a partner in crime, explain how the trick works and prepare a keyword to use that only the two of you know about.

① Announce to your class that you have telepathic powers. To prove your point, you will leave the room while the class, or a single volunteer, chooses an object from the room and tells your partner what it is.

② When you return, your partner will ask you what object the volunteer is thinking of – 'Could it be the lamp?', 'Is it the window?', 'Or is it the green plant?'. Consider each of these questions, as though connecting with your powers, but to each answer, 'No.'

③ Then your partner asks, 'Is it the red chair?' You answer 'No,' but they have alerted you with the word 'red'. This is the keyword that you have chosen, and when your partner uses this keyword you know that the next question they ask will be the right answer. 'Is it the picture on the wall?' your partner asks next, to which you reply, 'Yes'.
'It was!' gasps the astonished class. And you take your bow.

Pick five or six keywords and alternate between them ('red', 'big', 'on the table' etc.). Or use signals such as the way your partner points or the way you enter the room – putting three fingers round the edge of the door could signal to your partner to say the correct object on his third question. Your class will never be able to spot how the trick works and your answers will always be correct.

HOW TO VANQUISH A VAMPIRE

So you have suspicions about your neighbour, the one who never seems to come out during the day. He is tall, thin and pale, with smoothly combed black hair. He has a whispery voice, with a foreign accent, and when he speaks he covers his teeth. Could he have something to hide? You had better do some checking.

① Choose a bright sunny day to approach his house, scatter garlic bulbs around his front door then retreat to a safe hiding place. Wait until he comes out, and then watch his reaction. If he looks startled and heads rapidly back indoors, you might be on to something.

② Return to his house with a large mirror. Stand in a hidden spot where you can see his front door reflected in the mirror. When the door opens, can you see him in the mirror? If he has no reflection, he could be a vampire.

③ If all signs point to him being a vampire, you must take action. Arm yourself with lots more garlic, a crucifix, a sharpened wooden stake, and a bottle of holy water (if you have a spray bottle so much the better). Finally collect a small group of carefully chosen helpers, who should be similarly armed.

④ With your trusty companions, make your way into the vampire's basement and find his coffin. Be prepared in case a werewolf or other monstrous creature comes out from the shadows to defend his master.

⑤ The vampire wakes up and rises from his coffin, showing his fangs, trying to get them into your neck.

⑥ You and your friends surround him. You are so well supplied with garlic and other vampire deterrents that he is weakening rapidly. As the vampire cowers, it is time for you to strike.

⑦ Hold your stake firmly in your hands, aim for where the vampire's heart would be if he had one, and plunge! The vampire crumbles into dust before your eyes.

Be sure to test your vampire before you send him into eternal darkness – chances are he's just a quiet man with bad teeth!

HOW TO WRITE A SECRET MESSAGE

All top secrets are best kept and passed in code. Devising your own code to use with a friend is the best way of ensuring no one will crack it:

① Break your message into groups of two letters:
> I am the best at everything
> ia mt he be st at ev er yt hi ng

② Then reverse the letters in each pair:
> ai tm eh eb ts ta ve re ty ih gn

③ Now run the letters together:
> aitmehebtstaveretyihgn

Think about how you could adapt this code: adding a dummy letter between each pair of letters, swapping adjacent pairs, or reversing every other pair.

HOW TO READ A COMPASS

orienting mark   compass needle

direction-of-travel line

compass housing
(which can be turned)

base plate   compass dial

① Hold the compass flat in front of you so as to allow the compass needle to float freely. Assuming there is nothing magnetic close by, the needle will point to magnetic north. (Do make sure there's nothing magnetic about, though – if, for instance, you had a magnet in your pocket the needle would point to that instead of to the north. Large metal objects – an iron gate, for instance – can also affect magnetic compasses.)

② Rotate the compass housing until the orienting mark – N (for north) or the 0° symbol – lines up with the needle, making sure that it is the north end of the needle (indicated by a distinguishing mark – say by its being red) and not the south end hovering above the N or 0° mark.

③ Now you know where the magnetic north lies, which means that you now also know where south, east, west and all the other compass points are.

④ To use the compass to find your way to, say, a distant

hill, aim the base plate of the compass so that the direction-of-travel line points exactly at the hill.

⑤ Turn the compass housing until the orienting mark is beneath the north end of the compass needle, then double-check to make sure that the direction-of-travel line is still pointing at the hill. You now have your bearings – and if you have taken them accurately, by following the direction-of-travel line while keeping the compass needle over the orienting mark, you will reach the hill, even if you can no longer see it.

HOW TO FALL WITHOUT HURTING YOURSELF ...

...much

① Try to relax and not fight the fall – unless it is clear that falling would lead to serious injury (e.g. if there are unfriendly hazards like rocks or heavy machinery). In that case try to send your body the other way.

② Try not to land hands down as you could injure your wrists, elbows or shoulders.

③ Attempt to fall on your side rather than your front or back. Half-turn or roll if necessary to land on the fleshier parts of your body.

④ Don't allow your body to open out. Tuck up instead – chin firmly against chest, arms bent at the elbows to protect your head and face.

⑤ If you're on a bicycle, let go of it, try to swing your leg from under the bike and push the bike away from you.

HOW TO TAKE THE BEST PHOTOS

① The most interesting photos capture a moment that might never happen again. As such moments can rarely be planned, try to keep your camera within easy reach.

② When taking a photo of a person or animal, try to get a feeling of life and immediacy by establishing eye contact – or rather eye-to-lens contact.

③ Manual focusing can produce excellent results but quite often things change while you're still fiddling and the moment is lost. Automatic focusing is quicker but will assume that the object in the middle of the frame is what you wish to have in focus – what's behind, in front and to the sides will not come out as clear. You might be able to lock the focus. To do this: you first centre the subject of your picture in the frame and then press and hold the shutter button halfway down. Then, still holding the shutter halfway down, you change the position of your camera so the subject is framed how you want it to be. Then press the shutter button to take the picture.

④ Some cameras have an automatic flash – this can be annoying if you are trying for an artistic shot using low-level lighting. Again, it might be possible to override automatic flash. With many, though, the flash is manual – so remember to set it when it is needed.

Avoid taking photos too close up with a flash as the subject will appear bleached. The other common flash problem is 'red eye' in which the light is reflected off the back of the subject's eye. Some cameras have a red-eye reduction feature (with two flashes, the first to make the pupils smaller, the second to light up the subject). If yours does not, you could try flashing a bright light in your subject's face just before pressing the shutter (warn them first, though).

⑤ Visualize your photos as a whole. Look at the surrounding area – rather than just your subject. Choose your location carefully, check the background, remove or add items if necessary. Adjust lighting (there might be bright sun pouring through the window straight into your lens, or too little light).

⑥ Note that the morning or evening sun gives the most attractive light – in the middle of the day it can be too glaring. If you are taking a photograph in sunshine, be sure that the sun does not fall upon your lens. You might find that sunlight takes colour and definition from a subject's face – or exaggerates certain features.

⑦ With landscape, lighting is perhaps even more important than the location – in soft dawn light a view of a river curving through a field is beautiful, in the noonday sun it is flat and glaring, in the light of a sunset it is dramatic.

⑧ Experiment with taking photos from different angles. You do not have to be standing at eye-level – kneel down, or climb up on something to find the best perspective.

⑨ As always practise is the key. For this reason a digital camera is probably the best as you can see and keep or reject your photos instantly.

HOW TO JUGGLE

① Take one ball and throw it from hand to hand. Make sure each throw goes straight up and to the same height (to about eye level). Catch the ball at waist level.

② Now move on to two balls, one in each hand. Throw the first ball, A, just as in step ① above. Wait until it is about to descend and then throw the second ball, B, up underneath the first. If you can't react quickly enough at first, try throwing the balls higher to give yourself more time to catch them. If you find the balls are going forwards, throw them slightly in, towards yourself. Continue practising with the two balls until you feel confident. Then practise starting with your second hand.

③ Now for three balls. Start with two balls in one hand – ball A between your thumb, first and middle fingers, and ball C between your ring, little finger and the butt of your thumb. Ball B is in your other hand.

④ Throw ball A up; when it reaches its highest point, throw ball B.

⑤ Catch ball A.

⑥ When ball B reaches its highest point, throw ball C.

⑦ Catch ball B.

⑧ When ball C is at its highest point, throw ball A.

⑨ Catch ball C. Throw A up. And so on.

Now increase the height of your throws. Always have at least one ball in the air, and never more than one in either hand. Watch the balls as they reach their highest point and don't reach up to them, let them come down to you.

HOW TO SAVE THE WORLD

① Walk or cycle to school instead of being driven.

② Save electricity by switching off appliances when you are not using them.

③ Recycle everything you can – either by reusing items for other purposes or by taking them to recycling banks.

④ Throw litter into litterbins.

⑤ Take an interest in environmental issues: on television, in newspapers and on the Internet.

⑥ Take out reusable bags when shopping.

⑦ Take quick showers instead of deep baths.

⑧ Use energy-efficient light bulbs.

HOW TO MAKE A SQUEALER

The high-pitched squeal that some young animals make when in need will attract their mother as well as predators and other merely curious animals. You can make a device that imitates this squeal out of a hazel twig, and use it to see what animals you can attract.

You will need: one straight length of dry hazel twig about 2cm (¾in) thick and 16cm (6ins) long, a pocket knife with a strong sharp blade, three strong rubber bands – one of which must be approximately 9cm (3½ins) long by 4.5mm (³⁄₁₆in) wide unstretched.

① Trim the ends of the hazel twig and cut off any minor twiglets and bumps.

② With the knife (mind your fingers!), split the twig lengthways into halves. To do this, stand the twig on one end and rest the blade of the knife across the other end so as to bisect it. Press down on the knife blade until it has started to cut; then, holding the knife handle, tap the blade repeatedly with a piece of wood as it moves down through the twig.

③ Take one half of the twig and mark its centre. Then with the knife cut across the width of the twig half at two points, each about 2cm (¾in) from the marked centre, to a depth of about 1.5mm (¹⁄₁₆in). Using the knife, carefully scrape out the wood between the two cuts. You should now have one half of the twig with a shallow dip, 4cm (1½ins) long, across its centre.

④ Repeat with the other half of the twig, making sure that the two ends of each half-twig match, so that they will fit together again.

⑤ Take the longer rubber band and stretch it lengthways along one half of the twig, so that it lies flat and runs over the centre of the cut in the middle. Then place the two halves of the twig back together, trapping the long rubber band running between them.

⑥ Bind each end of the twig with one of the other shorter rubber bands, making as many turns as necessary to keep the twig halves firmly together.

⑦ Hold the twig across your mouth with your lips over the cut in the centre. Blow gently. Provided the rubber band trapped in the cut is tight enough, the effect should be a high-pitched but surprisingly loud squeaking sound, caused by the air passing over the stretched rubber band. You can experiment with variations of the note by adjusting the tension of the long rubber band: tighter = higher pitched; looser = lower pitched.

⑧ Blow for about two–four seconds; the harder you blow the louder and, to a limited extent, the higher the pitch; ending the call with a short hard blast will produce a high-pitched squeal, as though a young animal was in immediate danger.

⑨ Conceal yourself in a hedge, ditch etc. In this way, depending on where you are, you might attract roe deer, rabbits, foxes, badgers, hedgehogs, local cats and dogs – as well as curious or annoyed neighbours.

HOW TO REPAIR A BICYCLE PUNCTURE

① You'll need a puncture-repair kit, the bike manual and any necessary tools. Check the tyre for obvious causes of the flat – e.g. a nail or piece of glass. Now unscrew the valve to let any remaining air out of the tube, and take off the wheel. Then remove the tyre carefully so as not to pinch the tube. Pull the tube out, pressing the valve through the hole in the rim (if it is secured with a rim nut, unscrew that first). You can leave the tyre partially on the wheel.

② Look for the puncture. If it is not obvious, replace the valve, pump the tube up a little and listen for the hiss of escaping air, or dunk it in water. A stream of bubbles will reveal the site of the puncture.

③ Once you've found the puncture draw a circle round it. Making sure that the tube is completely dry, lightly roughen the area round the puncture with fine sandpaper. This will allow the glue to bond better – don't be tempted to skip this step.

④ Apply a thin coat of rubber solution over the area where the leak is, covering an area slightly larger than the patch. Allow it to dry completely – 3–5 minutes (patience!) – if you don't, the patch will probably come off.

⑤ Take a patch of the right

size and put a tiny blob of solution on its contact surface, then at once wipe off with your finger all but a very thin coat. Wait another 3–5 minutes. Then apply the patch, with the centre over the puncture, in one go (don't try to pull it off and reposition it), smoothing it down to get rid of any bubbles of trapped air, and press firmly.

⑥ Keep pressing it down really hard for at least a minute, especially round the edges. Wait for a couple of minutes and then carefully peel the backing paper or plastic off the patch. If an edge of the patch lifts with it, quickly press it back down; then try lifting the backing again from the other side. If the whole patch comes away with the backing, you'll have to start again with a new patch. (Self-adhesive patches do exist – but they do not always work very well.)

⑦ Once you've removed the backing, press down on the patch to seal the edges – then it's time to replace the inner tube. Dust it with French chalk (from your puncture repair kit – grate it on your sandpaper), especially all round the patch so it doesn't stick to the inside of the tyre. That done, replace the valve and pump a little air into the tube; this makes it easier to replace.

⑧ As you replace the tube, make sure the valve stem is correctly positioned and that the tube is not pinched or creased. If everything looks okay then pump the tyre up to normal pressure and put the wheel back on your bike. Inflate the tyre to the correct pressure.

You've done it – but keep an eye on that tyre for a while.

HOW TO BUILD THE BEST SNOWMAN

Forget the wonky heaps of snow with stones and twigs stuck in them ... charm and impress your friends and neighbours with the best snowman on the street.

① Check that the snow is of good consistency, and clumps together easily and isn't too wet.

② Take a handful of snow and compact it into a ball as you would to make a snowball for a snowball fight. Roll this ball along the ground so that more snow sticks to it, packing the snow by pressing it on with your gloved hands. Bring it to a standstill at the place you want the snowman to be. By now it is very large and heavy.

③ Repeat for your snowman's middle section and for his head. The bottom should be the biggest ball, and the head the smallest.

④ Pack some extra snow between the layers to make them stick together.

⑤ You have made the basic snowman shape. Now to give him an identity:

Arms: insert a couple of sticks on either side of his body and secure old gloves on the ends with elastic bands.

Face: eyes – coal, buttons or small round stones or goggly eyes from a joke or craft shop; nose – a carrot, fir cone or old Red Nose Day nose; mouth – a twig or row of small, dark stones; hair – a mop head, coloured string or an old plant.

Lightly spray your snowman with coloured water to give him rosy cheeks.

His wardrobe: dress your snowman with a hat and scarf. Insert three round stones down his front for jacket buttons and place boots at his bottom for legs.

For company, you could make an entire snow family, complete with a snow dog. But remember not to get too attached – your snowman's days are numbered. Make sure everybody sees your handiwork before the sun comes out.

HOW TO TIE A KNOT WITHOUT LETTING GO OF THE ENDS

① Lay a length of string on a table. Then fold your arms and, keeping them folded, take an end in each hand.

② Unfold your arms. And there's the knot!

HOW TO MAKE A WATERBOMB

Start with a square piece of paper.

① Fold in half across the middle in both directions, then unfold.

② Turn over. Fold in half from corner to corner in both directions, then unfold.

③ Fold along creases.

④ Fold corner to corner. Repeat behind.

⑤ Fold corner to centre. Repeat behind.

⑥ Fold corner to centre. Repeat behind.

⑦ Fold then unfold.
Repeat behind.

⑧ Using the creases
made in step ⑦, tuck
the small triangles in
the pockets (between
the layers) of the
larger triangles.
Repeat behind.

⑨ To inflate
the waterbomb,
blow into
the hole
at the
bottom.

blow

When it is finished your
waterbomb should look like
this. Fill it up, and give your
friend a good soaking!

HOW TO WRITE A LETTER

(1) Start with your address at the top right of the page. Below it, to the left, put the name and address of the person you are writing to. Put the day's date on the line below that and on the right-hand side of the page.

(2) Below and to the left, address the person you are writing to. If you know the person well, start with:
– 'Dear/Dearest Daddy' (or similar).
If the letter is more formal, start with:
– 'Dear Mr/Mrs Smith', or 'Dear Sirs/Dear Sir or Madam'.

(3) Leave a line and on the next line, starting at the left, begin writing your letter. Remember to use paragraphs and always check your spelling – get into the habit of using a dictionary. Whether you are typing or writing by hand, make sure the page is nicely spaced.

(4) End your letter on a new line to the left or the centre. If it is to a parent or friend close your letter with:
'Love from', 'With love', or even 'Hugs and kisses'.
If it is to someone you don't know quite as well leave it at:
'With affectionate greetings' or 'With best wishes'.
'With best wishes' can also be used to finish more formal letters, often followed by sign-offs, such as:
– to someone whose name you know: 'Yours sincerely';
– to someone whose name you do not know (i.e. Sir or Madam): 'Yours faithfully'.

(5) When addressing the envelope, make sure it is clear and readable, and use a different line for each separate part of the address.

HOW TO TELL IF A PERSON IS LYING

As the person is telling you his or her version of events, keep your ears and eyes open for tell-tale signs.

① Unusual stuttering or stammering could be an indication that the person is lying and may suggest that they are nervous.

② Note any changes in the person's pattern of speech. See if they seem high-pitched, put on a silly voice, speak particularly quickly or slowly, or use unusual words. For instance, does it sound as though the person has learnt their story off by heart?

③ Watch out for visible signs of stress or nervousness – sweating, twitching, scratching, rubbing, looking away, shifting around, crossing and uncrossing the legs, rapid breathing – all of these indicate that the person might not be telling the whole truth.

④ There are other signs to consider. Get the person to go over the story again – but not in sequence. Ask searching questions. Does he or she seem confused? Or apparently contradicting him or herself? Ask about unimportant details (along the lines of 'What colour was his T-shirt?'). Someone who is telling the truth is less likely to get muddled and anxious, even though they might have forgotten some of the details.

⑤ Some say that if the 'suspect', when questioned, looks to the left, they are inventing and if they look to the right they are remembering. Perhaps you could put this theory to the test.

HOW TO TURN CARTWHEELS

To perform a well-executed cartwheel you have to be quick and approach the turn with energy and confidence.

① Stand with your right leg in front, knees bent slightly and arms up straight.

② Reach forward and down with your right arm, throwing your left leg up as you do so.

③ Your left arm will follow very quickly, and as, or just before, it touches the ground, kick your right leg up in the air also. For a brief moment you are in a handstand.

④ Land with your right leg first, push with your hands, bring the other foot down and stand up straight. Try to keep a rhythm ('hand, hand, foot, foot').

If you find yourself flopping to one side before you have completed the cartwheel, you could try practising beside a wall, this will discourage your legs from going down in front of or behind you.

HOW TO BUNNY HOP

Being able to hop with your bike and lift both wheels off the ground is a great skill, especially when you need to avoid running over fallen friends who are trying to copy your cool trick.

Start by hopping the bike over a line on the ground, then move on to using a thin stick, and then steadily increase your hopping height. Don't forget to wear kneepads, elbowpads, gloves and a fitted helmet for safety. A BMX-style or mountain bike is easiest to use.

1. Stand on the bike's pedals.

2. Start pedalling until you get to about 8kph (5mph).

3. Lean the upper part of your body over the handlebars, keeping your weight centred.

4. Get your pedals level, so that your feet are parallel to the ground.

5. As you prepare for your hop, press down on the handlebars and pedals. Push your feet down, back, and then up, in one motion.

6. As you move your feet upwards, lessen the pressure of your feet and hands slightly but maintain contact between yourself and the bike. Crouch down on the bike.

7. Hop into the air.

8. Land as lightly as you can, taking the impact in your arms and legs, not your back.

HOW TO SHAKE OFF A TAIL

'A tail' is slang for a person secretly following someone else to observe their movements. Your first task is to find out if you are being followed, and if so, by whom. Your second task is to lose them.

Most amateur tails will follow behind you, trying not to be spotted.

① If you think you are being followed, occasionally stop as you walk around – perhaps to tie a shoelace, look for something in a pocket, admire something in a shop window, and so on. Casually scan people behind you – possibly on the other side of the road – and make a rough note of anyone within distance, especially such things as height, colour of clothes, type of coat etc.; look too for anyone you recognize from earlier on in your day. Stop again after a few hundred yards and take a casual glance round, as before – is there anyone still there?

② If there is, continue walking, but this time try going somewhere that most people would not go – use your ingenuity. Stop and look in shop windows, or pause to admire a shiny car or van (choose dark-coloured ones) – you can use the reflection on these surfaces to see who's behind you. Or pull out a comb and peer into the wing mirror of a parked car or motorbike, as though about to tidy up your hair – is there anyone whose reflection you recognize? If you're still not sure, try dawdling along and then suddenly stop dead (as though you'd suddenly forgotten something vitally important) and let everyone else walk past you – is there anyone a few yards back who has also stopped and who seems to be waiting?

③ Once you are certain you are being followed, make a note of what the person looks like. At the same time, make a plan for losing him or her.

④ First, change your own distinguishing features: if you're wearing a coat, take it off; if you're carrying a bag, hide it in your shirt; if you're wearing a hat, stuff it in your pocket, or if you've got a hat in a pocket, put it on.

⑤ Speed up: do this not by quickening your pace, but by lengthening your strides – if your pace is 30.5cm (1ft) long, and you lengthen it to 41cm (16ins), in 91m (100yds) you'll have travelled an extra 30.5m (33.3yds).

⑥ Dodge about: enter a large shop and immediately leave by another exit; go down a narrow alley and, while out of sight of your tail, sprint round a corner and double back on your tracks, resuming your normal pace once you're back on a main street. Jump on a bus just as it's about to shut its doors – the possibilities are endless.

⑦ As a last resort, hide: dodge about until you're out of your tail's sight; the moment you are, duck into a deep doorway, crouch down behind a parked car or a low wall, duck into the hallway of a large building – in short, anywhere that he or she will hurry past hoping to catch up with you again. Remember, your tail will be anxious not to lose you, and in that state of mind will probably overlook something right under his or her nose.

HOW TO LASSO LIKE A COWBOY

To make your lasso you will need about 10m (33ft) of stiff cord (the rope), a large needle and some thin string.

Take one end of the rope and make a small loop. It needs to be big enough for the rope to pass through it easily – but not much bigger than that. Instead of tying, sew the end of the loop to the rope with the string to make a permanent loop at one end. This loop is called a 'honda'.

Preparing and throwing the lasso:

① Take position in front of your target, a post or tree stump for instance. Pull the loose end of the rope through the honda. Stop when you have about 3m (10ft) left to feed through. This will be the loop you use to snare your target.

② Coil the loose end of the rope and hold it in one hand. Leave about 1½m (5ft) between the coil and the loop to allow you to swing your lasso.

③ Hold the loop-end of the rope in your free hand, about 20cm (8ins) from where the loop joins the honda.

④ Spin the lasso over your head with clockwise turns of your hand, tracing a circle in the air. Let your wrist act as an axle, and swing the rope as if it were a wheel spinning horizontally around your wrist and over your head.

(5) When you feel ready to rope your target, give a quick step forward, bring your hand forward and down to the level of your shoulder, let it stretch to a full arm's length without interrupting the swinging motion of the loop, and let it go at your target. The loop should sail straight at your target without losing its circular form.

(6) Now to snare the wild, kicking buffalo, or escaping cowboy criminal!

HOW TO MAKE A VOLCANO

This is a messy project and needs space, so if you can, make it outdoors or cover your work area with newspaper.

You will need: modelling clay (brown and red are best), baking soda, red food colouring, washing-up liquid, vinegar.

(1) Make a volcano shape with the modelling clay. Use brown clay for the base and red clay for the rim to look like hot lava. If you can't find red clay, colour a small amount with the food colouring.

(2) Scoop out a hole in the top of the volcano for the crater. Put 1 tablespoon of baking soda, a few drops of red food colouring and a few drops of washing-up liquid in the crater.

(3) Pour in ¼ cup of vinegar, stand well back and watch the volcano erupt!

HOW TO BOWL A SPINNER

Spin bowling is one of the most skilful bowling techniques in the game of cricket. The spin bowler uses the wrist and fingers to make the ball spin as it leaves the hand. The spin causes the ball to change direction once it lands. This makes it harder for the batsman to hit the ball, and can sometimes turn the ball from its path onto the wicket. In addition, a spinning ball may often come off the bat at an unpredictable angle, leading to the batsman being caught.

There are two main types of spin bowling – off-spin and leg-spin.

A few general tips: play with a cricket ball as often as you can – throw it up and down, twisting your wrist to make the ball spin in the air. Bear in mind that you can probably get more spin with a worn ball, so when playing a match try not to use a brand-new ball. When bowling, keep your arms close to your body. Bring your bowling arm down quickly and release the ball as high as you can, so the flight of the ball causes the batsman to lift his head up and then down, which may put him off his stroke.

Off-spin: twist your hand in a clockwise direction as you let go of the ball so that when it hits the pitch it will spin to your right. The spin is generated by the three middle fingers, with the middle joints of your fingers resting on the seam of the ball. As you bowl, turn your wrist in a clockwise direction to generate the spin on the ball. Then use your first two fingers to deliver the ball.

Leg-spin: twist the ball anti-clockwise and release it from the palm so that it rolls over the base of your little finger. It will spin to the left when it lands. Hold the ball with the top joints of the index and second fingers across the seam, the ball resting between a bent third finger and the thumb. As you release the ball, straighten your fingers; much of the work on the ball will be done by the third finger, turning the ball anti-clockwise. Flick your wrist so that your palm finishes facing downwards.

HOW TO FIND ORION

The constellation Orion, the Hunter, can be seen all over the world because it lies on the celestial equator. Even if you haven't identified them in the night sky, you may have heard of some of the stars that make up this constellation, including Rigel and Betelgeuse.

(1) Look towards the south if you are in the northern hemisphere, north if you are in the southern hemisphere.

(2) Find Orion's belt – three stars in a short, straight line.

(3) Look for Orion's knee to the lower right – it's the bright star, Rigel.

(4) Locate the orange-red star, Betelgeuse, at the upper left from the belt, often called 'Beetlejuice'.

(5) Scan the sky farther away to the lower left of the belt for the brightest star in the sky: the Dog Star, Sirius.

HOW TO CLIMB A ROPE

To most people, a long rope with no knots to grip looks impossible to climb. Here's how to escape the gym teacher and wriggle up the rope like a boa constrictor:

① Stand in front of the rope.

② Reach up with both arms – they should be well above your head, but slightly bent at the elbows to give you the necessary leverage.

③ Grasp the rope.

④ Pull yourself up.

⑤ As you do so, cross your legs round the rope and grip it between your thighs and again between your feet.

⑥ Reach up again, one arm at a time. Pull yourself up with your hands while using the grip between your feet and thighs to push up.

HOW TO BE A MATHS MAGICIAN

(1) Ask a friend to think of a three-digit number. The only condition is that the first digit and the last digit must differ by more than one – for example 364 would not do because there is a difference of only one between the first and last digits (3 and 4).

(2) Your friend might need a calculator – you, of course, do not. Now tell your friend to reverse the number. Let's say he or she chose 469 – reversing it would give 964.

(3) Now tell your friend to subtract the smaller number from the larger (964 - 469 = 495). All this is done without your knowing what any of the numbers are.

(4) Tell your friend now to take the result of this subtraction (495 in our example) and reverse it (594), and then to add the result and its reverse together.

(5) Your turn now. You announce the answer: 1089.

You will be right every time!

HOW TO WARM UP YOUR FEET

Sprinkle a pinch of ground cayenne pepper into your socks. It will warm your feet without burning them. But be sure that any cuts, blisters and scratches on your feet are covered with a sticking plaster, and be very careful not to allow the pepper to touch your eyes, or the nose and mouth area, as it might sting or at least feel uncomfortably hot.

HOW TO FIND FOSSILS AND TREASURE

'Local Schoolkid Finds Dinosaur Fossil,' announce the headlines above a photograph of you.

It could happen. Wherever you are, you may be standing on a fossil: perhaps bones, teeth, eggs, frozen mammoth flesh or fossilized fur. And there are other kinds of fascinating treasure to discover too, such as Bronze Age artefacts, Roman coins, jewellery and pottery.

There are often reports of people making such discoveries. A man on holiday, walking beside Loch Ness, tripped and fell – as he was getting up he spotted what turned out to be the fossilized section of a plesiosaur. Another man, as he strolled past a cliff, found himself suddenly staring at a small face in the rock. It turned out to be a 24,000-year-old carving, probably Neanderthal.

So you don't have to be an archaeologist or palaeontologist to uncover the remains of ancient life – you just need to be observant, patient and lucky.

Where to look:

① Beaches. Look in the shingle and under rocks as well as in the sand; if there are flints check them, too – they could contain fossils.

② Riverbanks. Check under stones and along the water's edge. Shallow streambeds are also worth investigating.

③ Cliffs. Erosion might uncover some super fossils (or Stone Age carvings), which you could find either in the cliff face or tumbled down to the foot of the cliff.

④ Quarries are a good place to look, where stone and earth has been dug up to use for building (but do observe safety precautions).

⑤ It's worth looking in farmland, too, especially fields where ploughing will have turned up the earth and all kinds of treasures that have been buried for years or centuries may have come up to the surface.

You will need tools to help unearth your fossils and treasure. Use a brush to remove gently any sand or soil, a small trowel to dig around your discovery, and a hammer and chisel if you are in a rocky area. Take kitchen paper with you to wrap your fossils, a camera to record your discoveries, and plastic bags so you can carry them to the museum!

HOW TO BEND IT LIKE BECKHAM

① Approach the ball at an angle. Place your standing foot (rather than your kicking foot) close to the ball, facing the direction you want the ball to go. Start by practising this as you go to kick the ball.

② Once you're comfortable with this, try to 'bend it'. If you kick with your right foot, to send the ball from right to left, strike the bottom half of the right-hand side with the inside, top half of your foot. To curve the ball from left to right, strike the bottom half of the left side of the ball with the outside of your foot. (Reverse these moves if you kick with your left foot.) To swerve a ball with the outside of your foot, strike 'across' the ball.

HOW TO MAKE A BOOMERANG

Boomerangs do not have to be single angled pieces of wood. They were traditionally that shape because they were made from bent pieces of wood. If you make one out of cardboard, an X-shape boomerang is far more effective.

You will need: cardboard, a ruler, scissors, glue or stapler, coloured markers (to decorate).

① Measure and cut two lengths of cardboard 20 x 3cm (8 x 1¼ins). Make sure the sides of each length are parallel and that the two lengths are identical to each other. Carefully cut the eight corners so that they are nicely rounded.

② Lay one piece across the other to form an X, crossing them in the centre and at right angles so that each wing of the X is the same length as the others.

③ Glue or staple them together at the centre.

④ Decorate your creation.

⑤ Fold up the end of each wing about 2cm (¾in) from the tip, to make a rough right angle.

⑥ To throw, hold your boomerang vertically by one of its blades so the folded tips bend toward you. Raise your arm and throw it with a quick snap of your wrist using just a little force.

(7) If it doesn't work after several tries, try adjusting the folded ends. You could also try placing four pea-sized blobs of Blu-tack on the underside of each wing about three-quarters of the length from the centre.

(8) Sooner or later, it'll whizz back to you every time.

HOW TO MAKE FIRE

(1) Rapidly twirling a dry twig round inside a hole in a plank of wood or a dead tree trunk will produce enough heat to set light to dry moss.

(2) Cutting a slot into a piece of bamboo and wearing down this slot with another piece of bamboo will work off fragments of the wood. The friction will set these shavings on fire.

(3) Striking a stone against a flint will create sparks which, if they fall onto dry moss, can set it alight.

(4) If it is bright and sunny you can set paper, dry moss or grass alight by holding a magnifying glass over it and drawing it upwards until the circle of sunlight the glass makes on the area is a tiny bright point. Hold it there and, as long as nothing comes between the sun and the magnifying glass, a tiny curl of smoke will soon appear, and then flames. (This is one reason why it is good advice not to leave glass bottles lying around in the countryside – these can start fires if the sun shines brightly on them.)

HOW TO DOWSE FOR WATER

Dowsing is a way of locating something that is hidden. A person – the dowser – using a rod, stick or other device known as a dowsing rod or 'wishing rod', can determine the exact location of such things as underground water, buried treasure, oil, lost objects and even people. Since the art of dowsing has never been scientifically proven, it is considered as a type of divination.

Traditional dowsing rods were made from forked hazel branches, although the wood of apple, beech and alder are said to work as well. Alternatively, L-shaped copper or iron rods are used. Or, unmystical as it sounds, wire coat hangers.

To make dowsing rods out of wire hangers, you need the long horizontal wire (the bit over which you might drape a pair of trousers) and about 10cm (4ins) of one angled side. Take two hangers and cut from them this angled length using a pair of wire cutters. Bend each of the short sides out a little to form a right-angle or L-shape. The shorter end is the handle: over each handle fit half a plastic drinking straw to form a sleeve (this allows the rod to swivel freely without being affected by your hand).

To dowse with your L-shaped rods, hold a rod in each hand, horizontally in front of you. When you're over water the rods will cross each other, apparently moving of their own accord, pointing towards the spot where the water can be found.

HOW TO MAKE A PRECIOUS GIFT FOR FREE

You can make attractive and unusual gifts in the form of small ornaments or paperweights. Your basic material is a good collection of nice smooth pebbles of different sizes and colours.

You will need: clear nail varnish, a foil pie dish, a scrubbing brush and washing-up liquid, newspaper, kitchen paper and water.

① Spread newspaper over your work area. Scrub your pebbles and stones well with the brush and washing-up liquid. Rinse thoroughly and let them dry out completely.

② Fill the pie dish with about 2cm (¾in) of water.

③ Let a drop of nail polish fall into the water. This will spread over the surface of the water, making a cellophane-like film.

④ Holding the pebble with your fingertips roll it slowly across the bottom of the pie tin, covering it in the film.

⑤ Put the pebble on the newspaper. When it is dry, you will have a beautiful, iridescent gemlike stone.

⑥ To go on to polish another one, first skim the left-over nail varnish off the surface of the water, then put in another drop and repeat the process.

⑦ Experiment by gluing small, pearlescent stones together, or using shells. Wait until the varnished stones are dry and use little drops of glue to stick your colourful gems together.

HOW TO JUMPSHOOT A BASKETBALL

① Start with both feet flat on the floor. With your body facing the basket, crouch down low – this will give you the momentum to jump.

② Rise up off your feet. Make sure you can see the rim of the hoop. Your shooting hand should cup the ball and point towards the basket, while your other hand can gently guide the shot, loosely holding the side of the ball.

③ Keep your elbows in and your eyes on a spot over the front of the rim. Bend the wrist of your shooting hand backwards, the ball resting on the pads of your fingers.

④ As you spring off the ground, extend your arms, raising the ball smoothly in one fluid motion.

⑤ At the top of the jump, snap your wrist forward to release the ball up.

⑥ At the end of the shot, when the ball flies through the hoop, your fingers should be pointing down to the floor.

HOW TO SPEED-READ

When you read, it is not necessary to look at every letter of a word to know what the word is; you don't even have to see the word in detail, as you know by its shape and length and by its context (the meaning of the rest of the sentence in which it appears) what it is. To speed-read you have to be able to scan the lines you are reading. The brain soon learns which words are the important ones and also learns to take several words in together.

To speed up your reading, run your finger along beneath each line you read. Gradually increase the speed of your finger and you'll find your reading speeds up too. Don't hurry this, though, or you just won't take in what you're reading.

To progress your speed-reading, use a newspaper, as columns are narrower than book pages. Draw a line right down the centre of a column. Now try to read each line without moving your eyes from the beginning to the end of the line but by looking at its centre. After a while you'll find that your eyes are taking in a complete line at a time – and if you continue, you'll find that your brain starts doing the same and you can fully understand what you're reading. After a while don't draw the line and you'll soon be able to read a newspaper column just by running your eyes down the centre.

Avoid saying the words to yourself, and going back over something you've just read. Doing so will slow you down.

HOW TO SURVIVE AN EARTHQUAKE

Fortunately the great majority of the earthquakes that are occurring around us nearly all the time are so slight that only seismographs register them. Stronger earthquakes, however, can cause a great deal of damage.

1. If you are indoors and have time, turn off all gas- and fire-related equipment (a gas fire or cooker, for instance). Stay indoors. Drop down to the floor and take cover under a strong table or desk. Hold on to it and, if necessary, move with it. Failing suitable pieces of furniture, stand in a doorway. Keep clear of windows, glass, fireplaces, and heavy furniture or appliances. Stay put until the shaking stops and it's safe to move.

2. If you're outside, if possible get out into the open. Stay away from buildings, trees, power lines, bridges, high walls and rocks.

3. If you're in a car, urge everyone to stay in the vehicle. Ask the driver to keep the car away from traffic, bridges, overpasses and tunnels, trees, lamp posts, power lines and road signs and to stop the car where it seems safe.

4. After the shaking has stopped, check for any injured people and make sure they're as comfortable and safe as possible; check for hazards – fire, water leakages, damaged structures – turn off power supplies if a gas leak is suspected or electrical wiring is damaged, and clean up dangerous spills. Only use the telephone for emergencies and keep listening to the radio. Expect aftershocks and even tidal waves (seismic sea waves).

The Richter Scale measures an earthquake's strength:

1–3	Generally not felt but recorded on seismographs
3–4	Felt, but damage very rare
4–5	Widely felt, some local damage, not significant
5–6	Damage to poorly constructed buildings
6–7	Destructive – a fair amount of damage
7–8	Major – serious damage over large areas
8–9	Great – widespread destruction and loss of life.
9–plus	Rare – causes great destruction over huge area

HOW TO LOCATE A THUNDERSTORM

Water droplets colliding inside storm clouds cause electrons to move so quickly that a large electrical spark is created. This is lightning. The air along its path is heated so intensely and expands so much that it creates a very loud noise – thunder. But although lightning and thunder occur together, we see the lightning some time before we hear the thunder because the speed of light is about a million times that of sound. It is possible to estimate how far away a thunderstorm is by counting the number of seconds between the lightning flash and the thunderclap. Divide what you get by three and that will give you the approximate distance in kilometres.

HOW TO ROW A BOAT

It is a good idea not to go off alone in a boat – take a friend with you. Make sure you are prepared – that you are both wearing life jackets and that the boat is in good condition.

① Sit with your back to the bow (the front of the boat) and your feet against the foot board, your legs slightly bent at the knee. Place an oar in each rowlock – the U-shaped metal fittings that fit into holes in the boat's side to hold the oars.

② If you have a companion, he or she should get into the boat and sit at the back – that is, on the stern thwart. Get him or her to push the boat off from the bank or jetty so that it drifts out.

③ With your arms straight out in front of you, hold the oar handles with your wrists dropped so that the oar blades are parallel to and just above the surface of the water. Keep your back straight and look directly in front of you, which, when you're rowing, is over the stern (the back of the boat).

④ Lower the blades into the water and, at the same time, straighten your wrists – this will set the blades at right angles to the surface as they enter.

⑤ Lean back and bring the oar handles towards your chest, completing the stroke by bending your arms. Your weight, and the effort of your legs, more than the strength of your arms, pull the blades through the water, making the boat move in the opposite direction. So you are effectively going backwards.

(6) As the stroke ends, lift the blades from the water, straighten your arms and lean forwards again – this will bring the blades back to the starting point again.

(7) Lower the blades into the water and take another stroke, and so on. The hardest strokes are the first six or seven; once the boat is actually under way, less effort is needed to keep it travelling at the same pace.

(8) Pulling harder on one oar will make the boat turn away from that side – i.e. if you pull on your right oar, the boat will move towards your left (which is to the boat's right, since you're facing backwards).

(9) To slow or stop the boat, drop the blades into the water and brace yourself against them – the flat blades will act as brakes. To move the boat backwards, hold that position and then push against the oar handles, so that the blades move through the water in the opposite direction. As the blades near the bow, lift them out of the water, lean back and drop them in again to take another stroke – in effect, rowing in reverse.

If for any reason the boat should be upset and you end up in the water – Don't panic! Your life jacket will keep you afloat. Stay close to the boat until help arrives or until you and your friend can push it to the bank by holding on to one side and kicking with your legs. You can climb back in provided your friend is holding on to the other side as you do so, to counterbalance your weight.

HOW TO TELL WHICH WAY IS NORTH

You will need: a wristwatch with hands, set to the correct local time. You need to be able to see the sun (even if it's shining through cloud). Most important of all, you also need to know that the sun rises in the east and sets in the west; and that at 12 noon in the northern hemisphere it is due south (in the southern hemisphere it's due north).

northern hemisphere

① With the watch horizontal, aim the hour hand at the sun. Then exactly divide the angle between the position of the hour hand and the 12 on the watch face – the line that follows that angle is the north–south line. Since you know the position of the Sun at noon, and you know the time, you can then work out which way is north and which south.

② If you have a digital watch, draw a watch face on a piece of paper, mark the 12 and then draw in the hour hand in the position for the time shown on your digital. Next, aim the hour hand in the drawing at the sun and follow the procedure as for a watch with hands (technically termed an analogue watch).

③ If you are in the southern hemisphere, aim the 12 on

the watch face at the sun and find the north-south line by bisecting the angle between the hour hand and 12. Remember that in this hemisphere, the sun will be due north at noon; otherwise, exactly the same principles apply as for the northern hemisphere.

HOW TO GET AN EGG INTO A BOTTLE

You will need: a peeled, hard-boiled egg, a plastic or glass bottle with an opening slightly smaller than the egg, and a large jug of hot water.

① To hardboil an egg put it in a saucepan, cover with water and simmer it for eight-ten minutes. Then put it in cold water and leave it for at least another ten minutes to cool down. When the egg has cooled down, tap it gently until the shell cracks. Peel it carefully. At the end you should have a smooth, unblemished white oval.

② Heat the bottle, inside and out, by filling it with hot water. Pour out the water and then quickly place the egg, pointed side down, in the bottle opening.

③ As the air inside the bottle cools, the egg will slowly move into the bottle.

④ To get the egg out, hold the bottle upside-down so that the egg is near the opening. Blow hard into the bottle with your mouth tight against the opening. The egg will vibrate, but then act as a seal, trapping air inside. Point the bottle away from yourself and watch the egg fly out!

HOW TO RIDE A UNICYCLE

① Get two friends to stand either side of you and get up on the unicycle with your arms around their shoulders. Check that the unicycle is the correct height by sitting on the saddle and placing one foot on a pedal at the lowest point. You should be able to reach that pedal with your leg very slightly bent.

② Sit up straight and look straight ahead. Your weight should be on the seat, not on the pedals. Rock the pedals to get a sense of balance, and then bring the pedals halfway round so that they're level.

③ Still holding on to your helpers, pedal a half-turn, then stop. Do this a few times before going on to pedal full turns. Doing lots of half-turns (from pedals level to pedals level again) is harder than continuous pedalling, but keeps you in control of the movement.

④ Switch from holding on to your helpers' shoulders to holding their wrists, and then to holding the wrist of just one helper.

⑤ Let go of both helpers and switch to using a wall instead. Pedal a half-turn forwards, sliding your hand along the wall. Build this up into a whole turn, two turns and so on until you are comfortable sliding along the wall and you are happy to have a very light hold of the wall.

⑥ To turn the unicycle, swivel your body and the unicycle in the direction you want to go, but be careful to avoid leaning to the side.

HOW TO DRAW A CARTOON

If you can draw a basic face shape, it is very easy to adjust certain features to give each of your cartoons a different personality. Start with a basic oval, then add other ovals for the nose and eyes. Then simply decorate with different-shaped mouths, and try moving the eyeballs or eyebrows, or adding hair or glasses. See what expressions you can create. You will soon begin to build a library of faces with different and hilarious personalities.

HOW TO BE THE BEST ALL ROUND THE WORLD

If you know many languages, you can be the best around the world ... or at least people will think you are!

English	I am the best
French	Je suis le/la meilleur/e
Russian	Ya velikiy/velikay
Spanish	Soy lo mejor
Italian	Sono il migliore/la migliora
Urdu	Māi sab se achā/achi hū
Portuguese	Sou o melhor/a melhora
German	Ich bin das Beste
Swedish	Jag är bäst
Danish	Jeg er den bedst
Greek	E-me o kaliteros/i kaliteri
Polish	Jestem wspaniały/wspaniała
Arabic	Ana Al'aadham
Mandarin	Wǒ shi zuì hǎo de
Hindi	Māi sab se achā/achi hū
Swahili	Mimi mbinga ni
Latin	Optimus/optima sum

Note: where applicable the masculine version is given first,
followed by the feminine after an oblique stroke.